RECORDED VERSIONS
GUITAR ®

AUTHENTIC TRANSCRIPTIONS
WITH NOTES AND TABLATURE

W9-APV-743

CREED
human clay

All artwork except for photographs © 1999 Wind-up Records Inc.

Music transcriptions by Pete Billmann, Colin Higgins, and Jeff Jacobson

ISBN 0-634-01397-1

HAL•LEONARD®
CORPORATION

7777 W. BLUEMOUND RD. P.O. BOX 13819 MILWAUKEE, WI 53213

Visit Hal Leonard Online at
www.halleonard.com

CREED
human clay

Contents

Photography by Kylie Bailin

Scott Stapp

Photography by Kylie Bailin

Mark Tremonti

Photography by Kylie Bailin

Brian Marshall

Photography by James Williams

Scott Phillips

Are You Ready?

Words and Music by Mark Tremonti and Scott Stapp

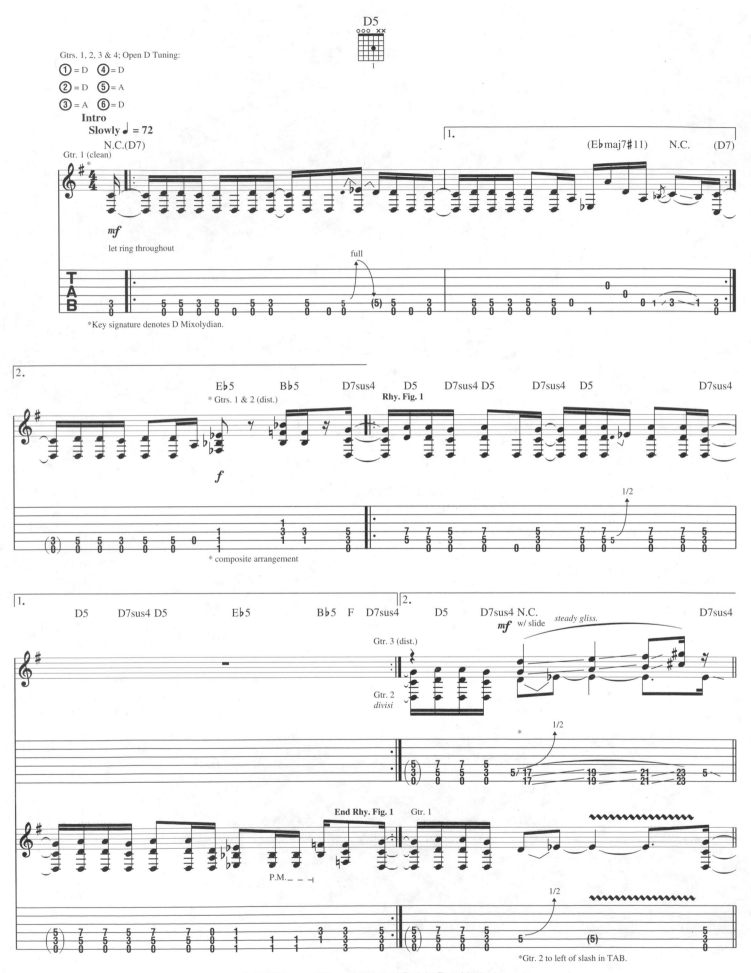

read - y? _____

Are you read - y _____ for us _____ to _____

_____ come?

Bridge

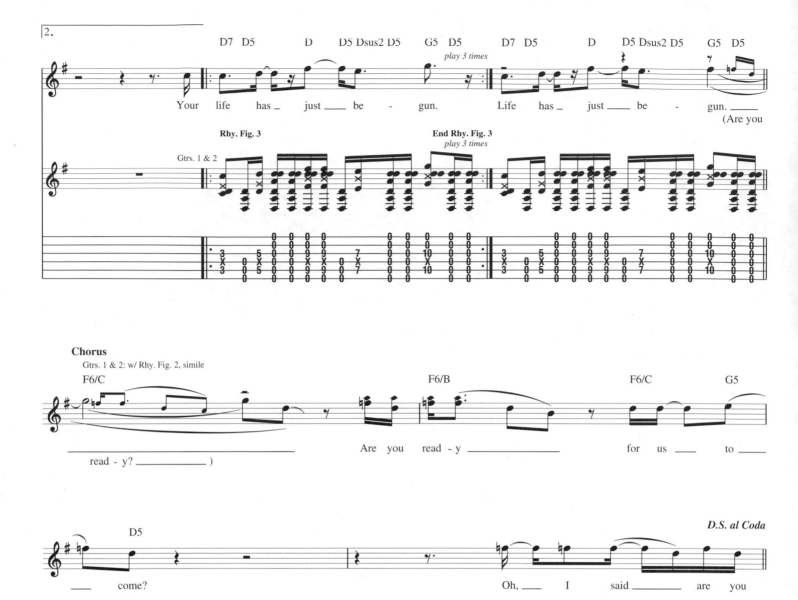

Chorus
Gtrs. 1 & 2: w/ Rhy. Fig. 2, simile

Coda

Outro

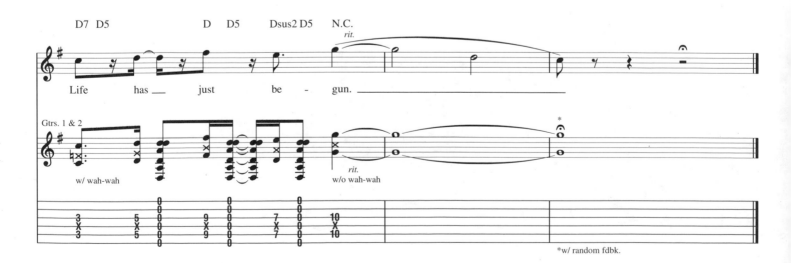

What If

Words and Music by Mark Tremonti and Scott Stapp

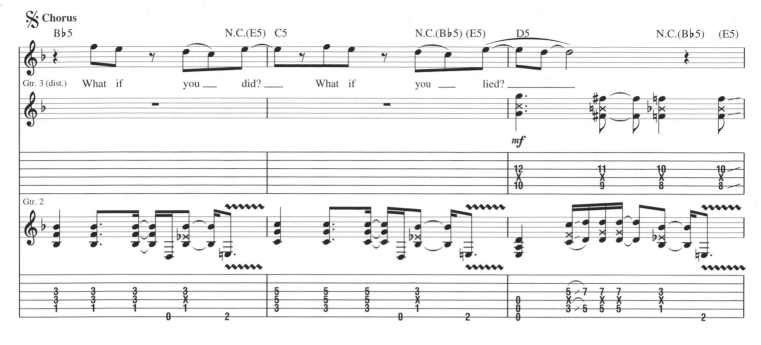

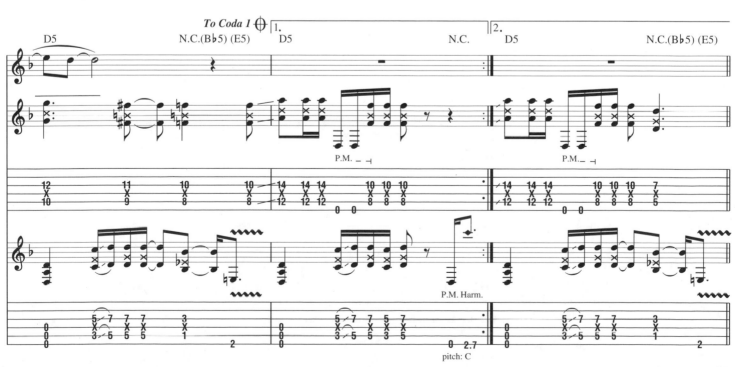

Beautiful

Words and Music by Mark Tremonti and Scott Stapp

Verse

Gtr. 1: w/ Riff A, 3 1/2 times, simile
Gtr. 4 tacet
N.C. (Dm)

3. In your mind she's your com-pan-ion. ___ Vile in-stincts of-ten can-did. ___

D.S. al Coda 1
Gtr. 1: w/ Riff B
Gtr. 2: w/ Rhy. Fill 1
D5 N.C.

___ Your re-gret ___ is all that's left. ___

Coda 1

me, ___ she stripped ___ me. ___

End Rhy. Fig. 2

Gtr. 2
Rhy. Fig. 2

P.M. 1/2 P.M. _ _ _ _ ⌐ 1/2 P.M.⌐ P.M.

1/2 1/2 1/2

Riff C End Riff C

1/2 1/2 1/2

Guitar Solo

Gtr. 5 (dist.)
Gsus2 * G Gsus2 D5

** < *mf*
† fdbk.
w/ E-bow

Gtrs. 2 & 3
* Rhy. Fig. 3

* Key signature denotes D Mixolydian.

** vol. swell
† Microphonic fdbk., not caused by string vibration.

Say I

Words and Music by Mark Tremonti and Scott Stapp

Guitar Solo

D5   Gtr. 1: w/ Rhy. Fig. 2, 2 1/2 times, simile

Rhy. Fig. 2   Eb5   D5   Eb5

Gtr. 1   **End Rhy. Fig. 2**

P.M.

Gtr. 3 (dist.)

mf
w/ delay   delay off

Bridge

Gtr. 3 tacet

D5   Eb5   D5

Fran - tic fo - cus._____ These things   un,
(Fran - tic fo - cus.   These things un -
Spoken: Frantic, faction, focus The world breathes and out this misconception We call man.

Eb5 D5

no hold on us. So look ___   in - side, ___   and you'll
hold   us. So look ___   in - side, ___   you'll
But I don't know him.   *I don't know him,*   *because he*

                   (cont. in slash)

Gtr. 1   *3*   Gtr. 3

                 Gtr. 1
                 divisi

P.M.

Interlude

Gtr. 1 tacet

D5

Gtr. 3

P.M.

see ___   they lie. ___
see ___   they _ lie. ___   )
Gtr. 1 *lies.*

                 Gtr. 2

P.M.   *mf* chorus off
              w/ fingers   let ring _ _ _ _ _

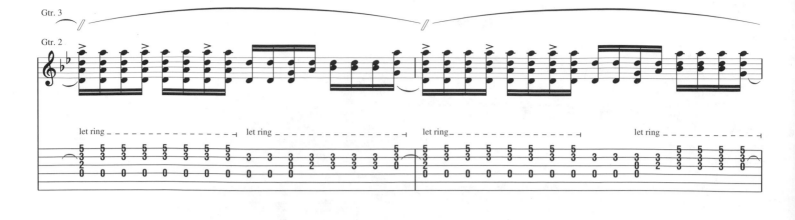

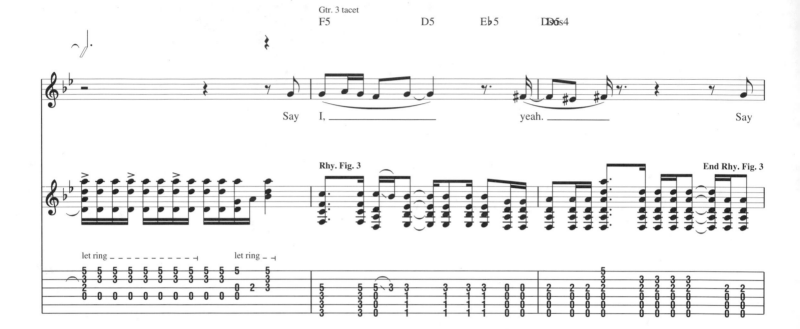

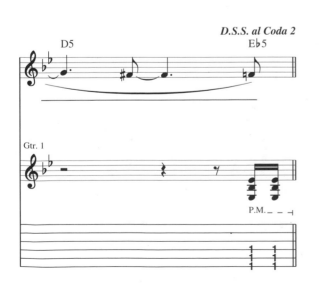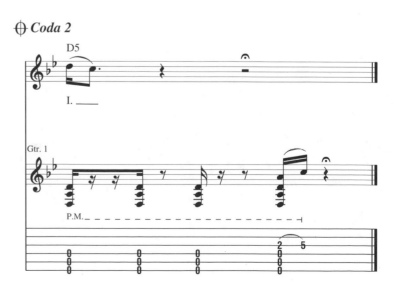

Wrong Way

Words and Music by Mark Tremonti and Scott Stapp

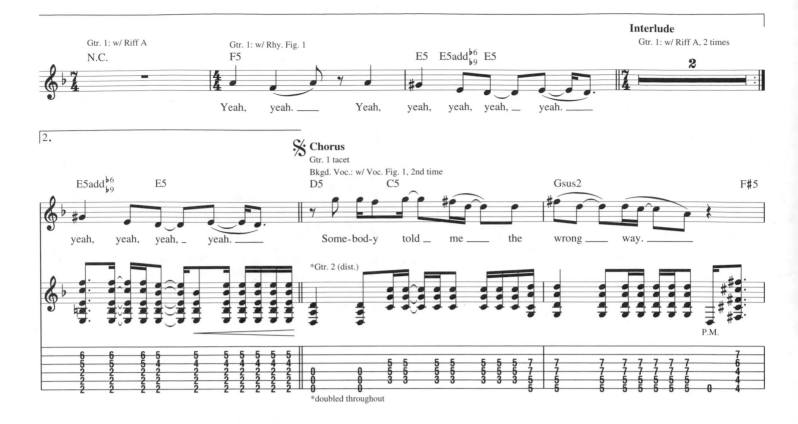

Bridge

Gtr. 2: w/ Rhy. Fig. 2, 1 1/2 times

What if I _____ died? _____

What did I _____ give? _____

(Yeah, yeah. Yeah, yeah.)

I hope it was an an-swer _____ so you might _ live. _

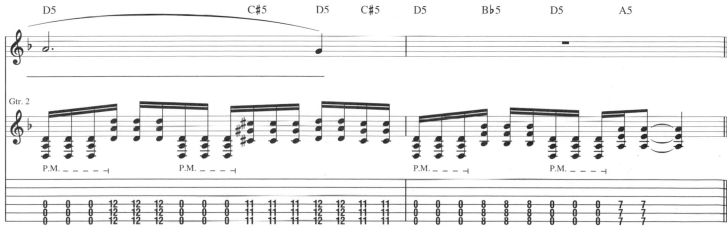

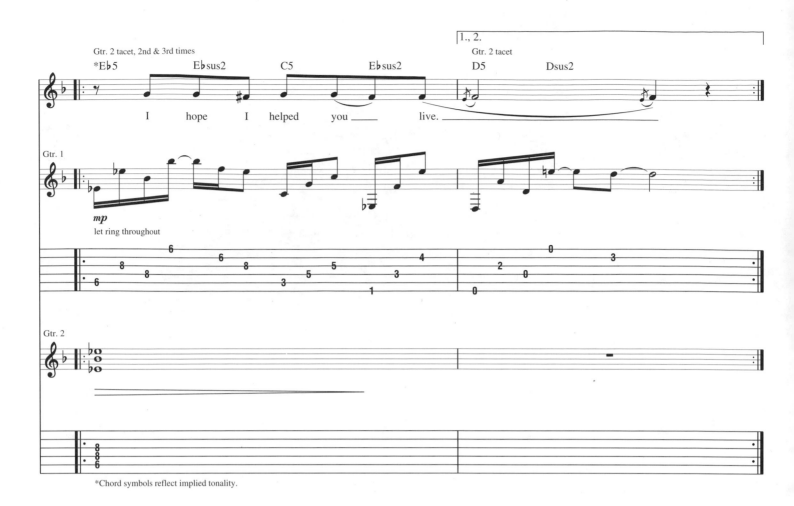

*Chord symbols reflect implied tonality.

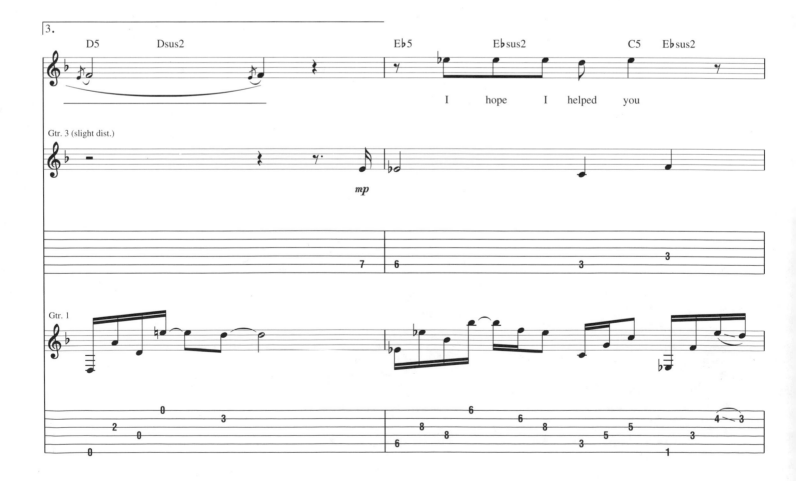

Faceless Man

Words and Music by Mark Tremonti and Scott Stapp

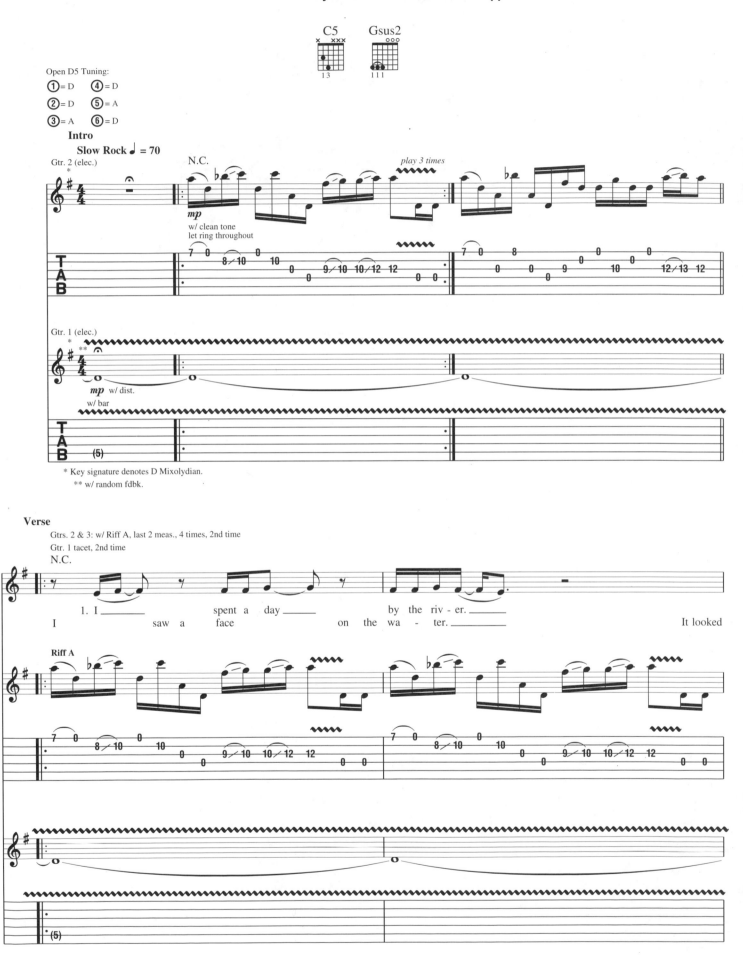

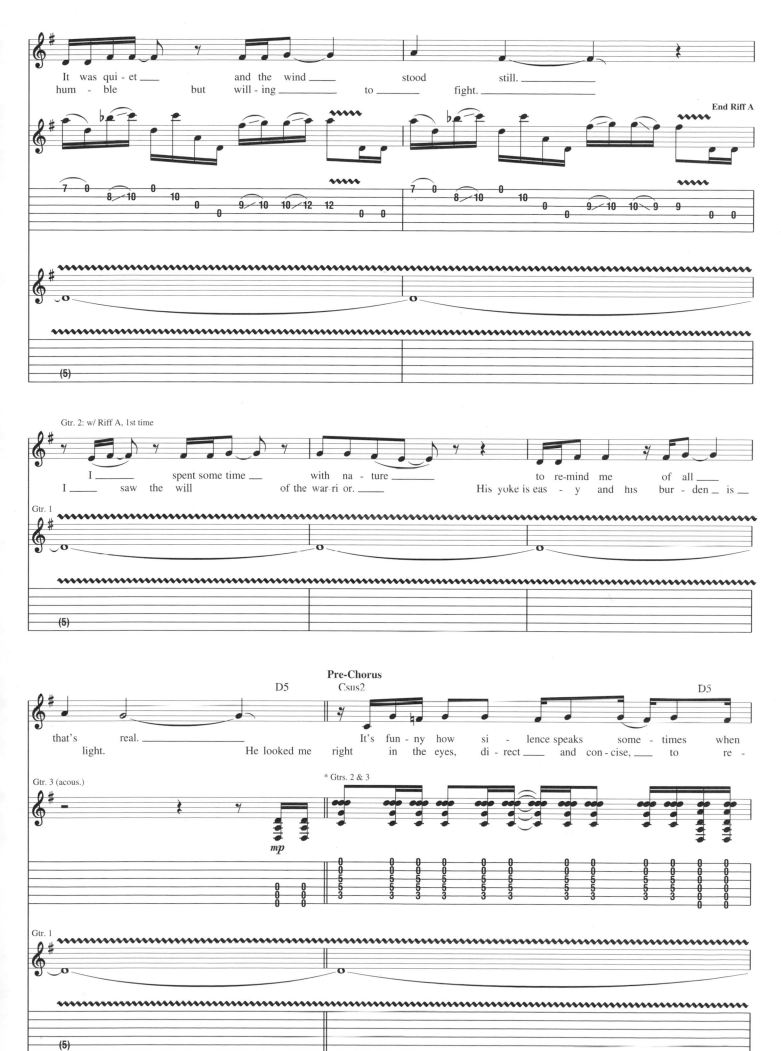

End Riff A

It was qui-et ___ and the wind ___ stood still. ___
hum-ble but will-ing ___ to ___ fight. ___

Gtr. 2: w/ Riff A, 1st time

I ___ spent some time ___ with na-ture ___ to re-mind me of all ___
I ___ saw the will of the war-ri-or. ___ His yoke is eas - y and his bur-den ___ is ___

Gtr. 1

Pre-Chorus

D5   Csus2   D5

that's real. ___ It's fun-ny how si - lence speaks some-times when
light. He looked me right in the eyes, di-rect ___ and con-cise, ___ to re-

Gtr. 3 (acous.)

* Gtrs. 2 & 3

mp

Gtr. 1

* composite arrangement

31

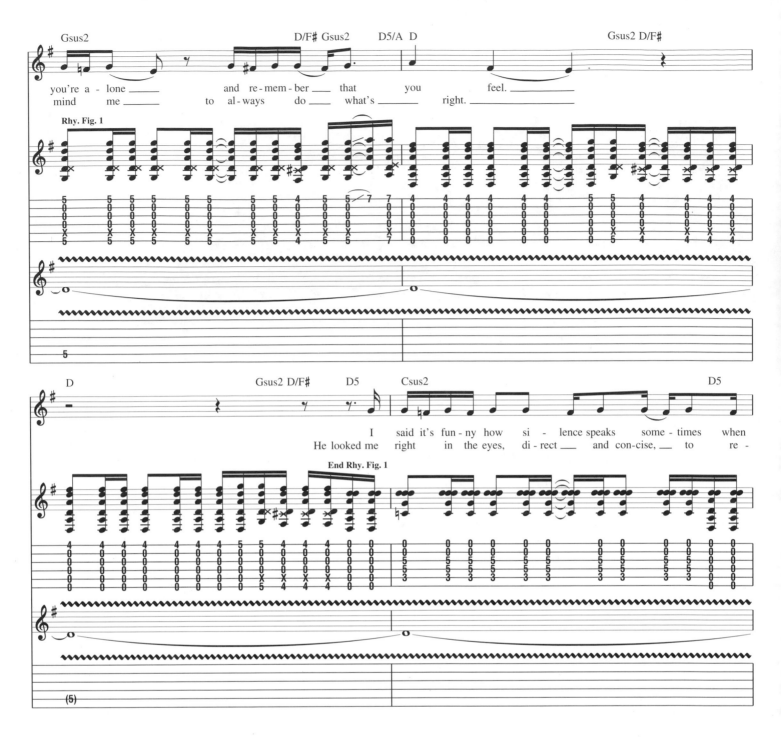
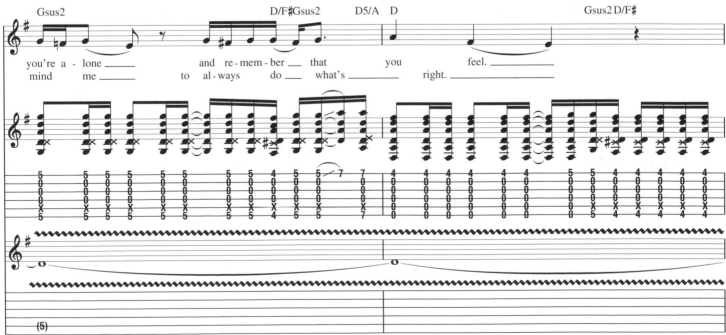

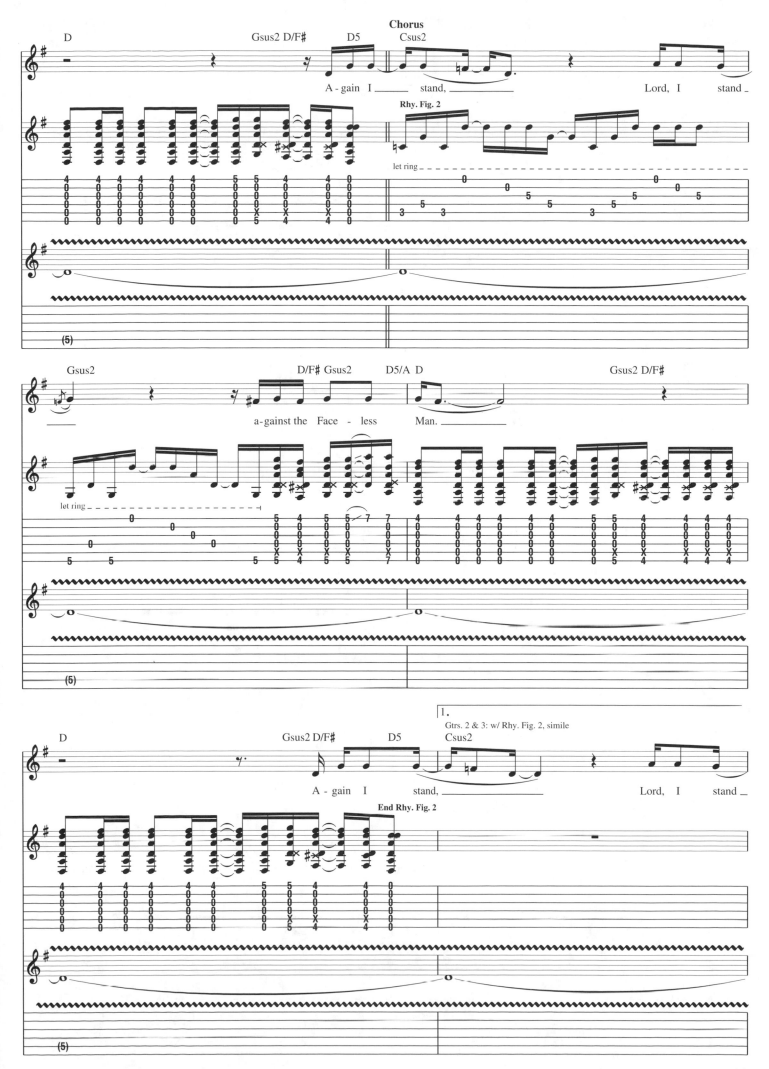

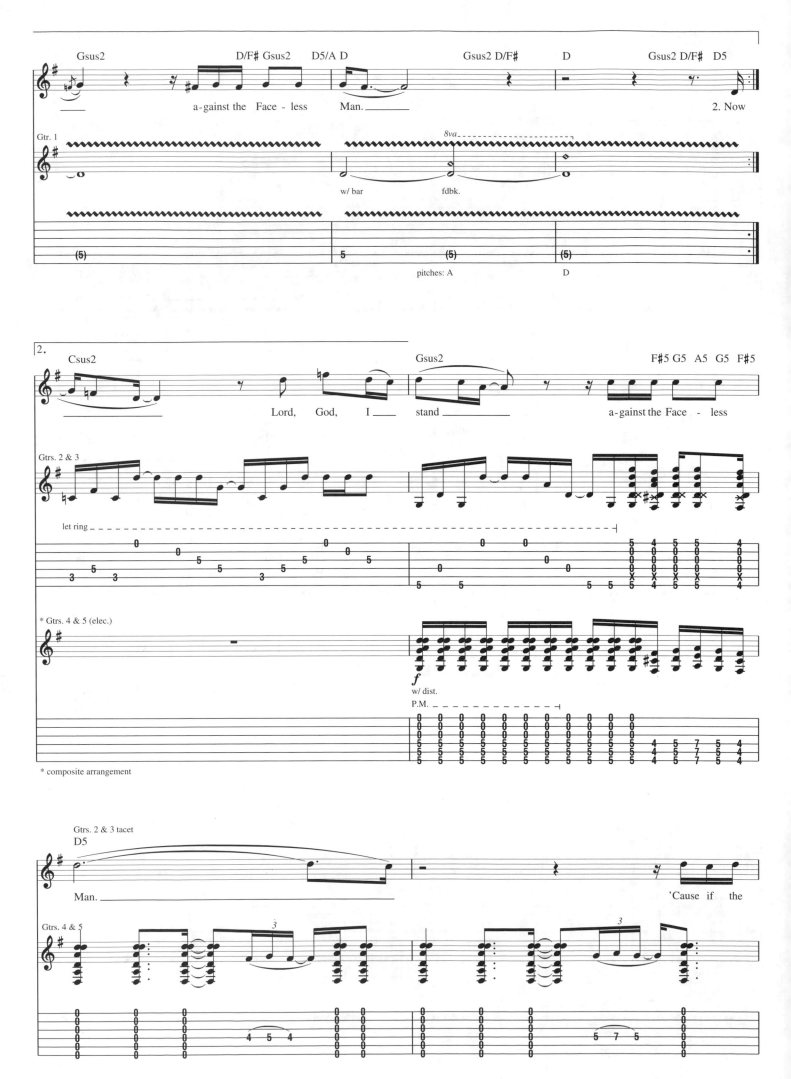

Interlude

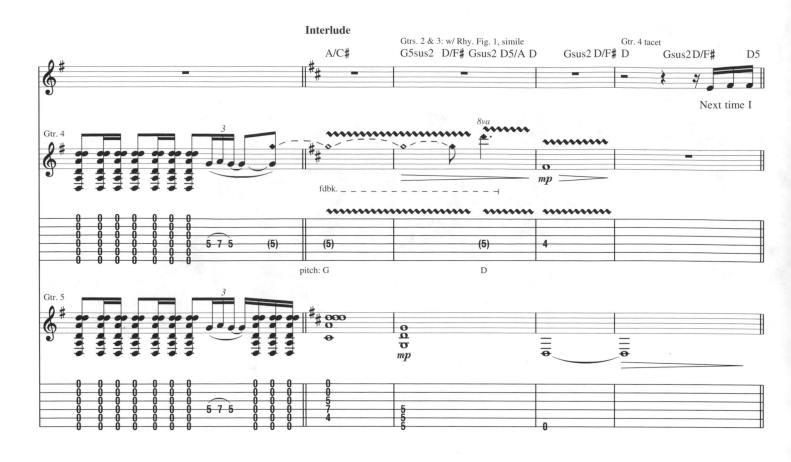

Next time I

Bridge

see this face

I'll say

I

* Chord symbols reflect overall tonality.

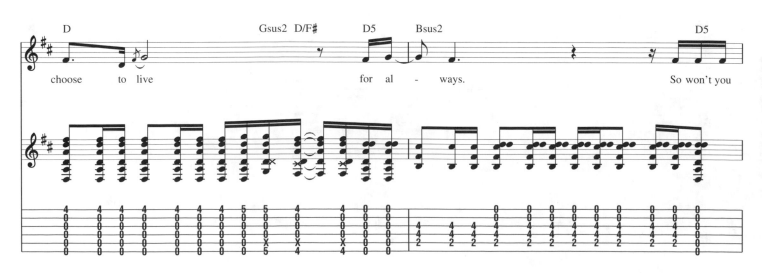

choose to live for al - ways.

So won't you

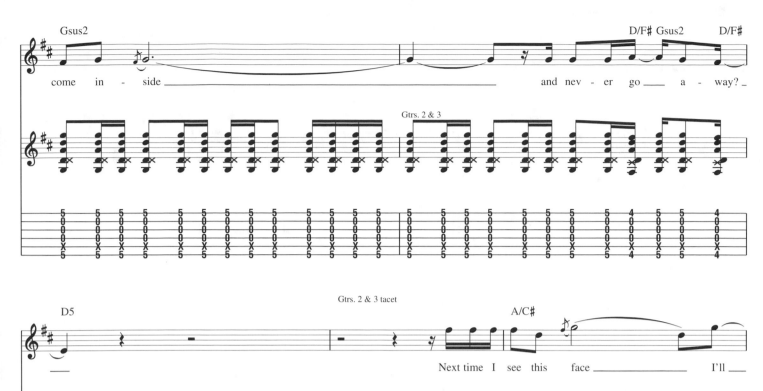

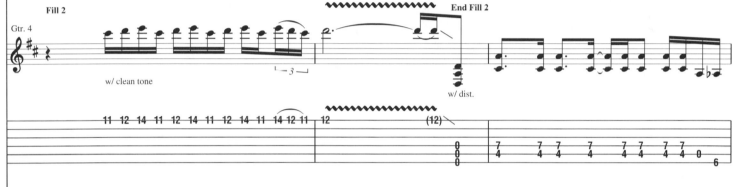

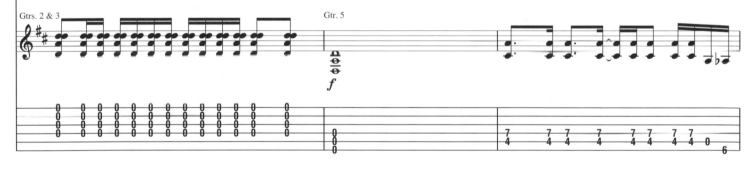

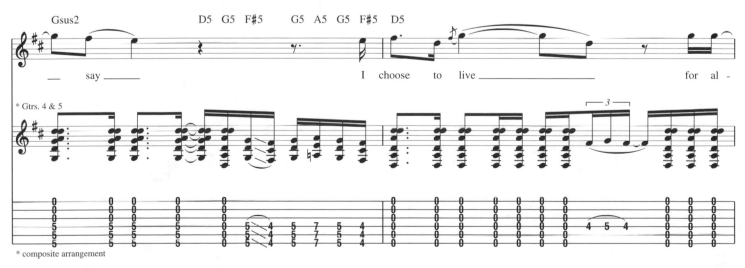

Outro-Chorus

Gtrs. 4 & 5: w/ Rhy. Fig. 3, 2 times, simile

Never Die

Words and Music by Mark Tremonti and Scott Stapp

nev - er

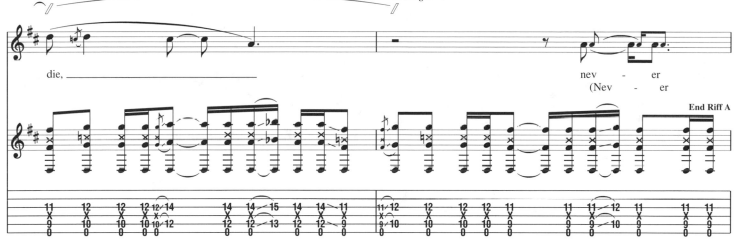

die, _____ nev - er
(Nev - er

Voc. Fig. 1

End Riff A

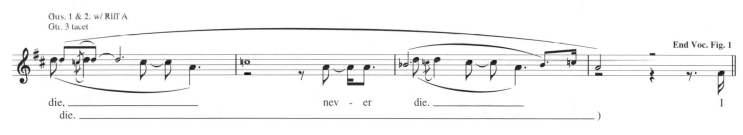

Gtrs. 1 & 2: w/ Riff A
Gtr. 3 tacet

End Voc. Fig. 1

die, _____ nev - er die. _____ I
die. _____)

Bridge

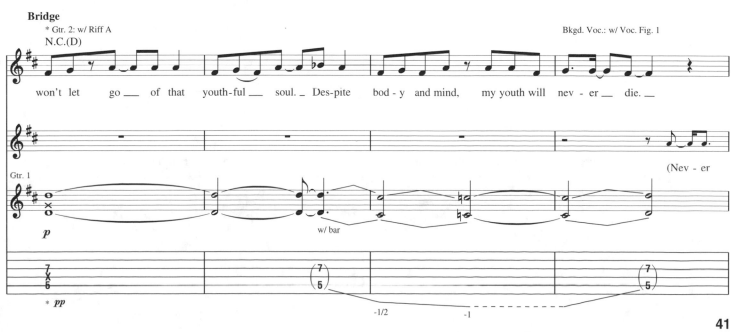

* Gtr. 2: w/ Riff A

Bkgd. Voc.: w/ Voc. Fig. 1

N.C.(D)

won't let go ___ of that youth-ful ___ soul. _ Des-pite bod - y and mind, my youth will nev - er ___ die. _

(Nev - er

Gtr. 1

p

w/ bar

* pp

-1/2   -1

With Arms Wide Open

Words and Music by Mark Tremonti and Scott Stapp

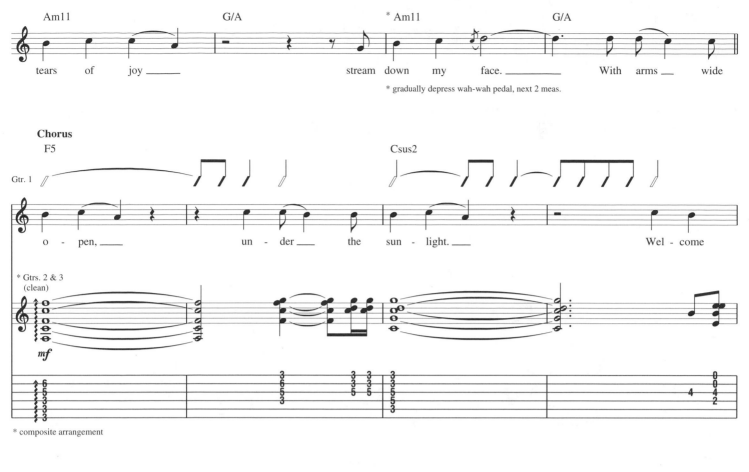

*gradually depress wah-wah pedal, next 2 meas.

tears of joy _____ stream down my face. _____ With arms _____ wide

Chorus

o - pen, _____ un - der _____ the sun - light. _____ Wel - come

* Gtrs. 2 & 3 (clean)

* composite arrangement

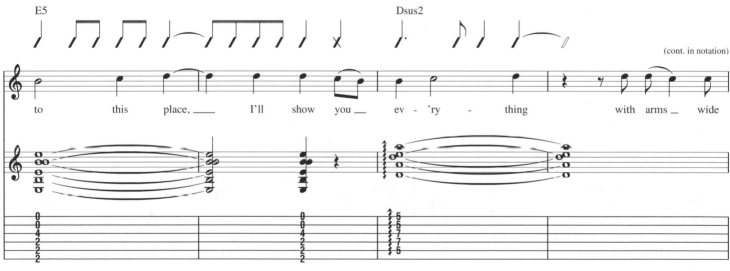

(cont. in notation)

to this place, _____ I'll show you _____ ev - 'ry - thing with arms _____ wide

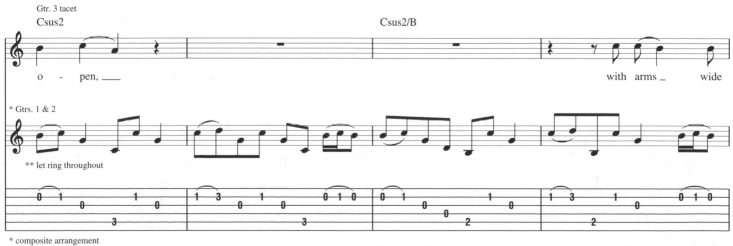

Gtr. 3 tacet

o - pen, _____ with arms _____ wide

* Gtrs. 1 & 2

** let ring throughout

* composite arrangement
  ** next 8 meas.

Verse
Gtr. 1: w/ Riff A, 2 times, simile

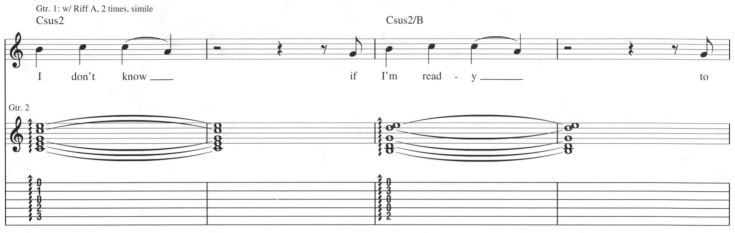

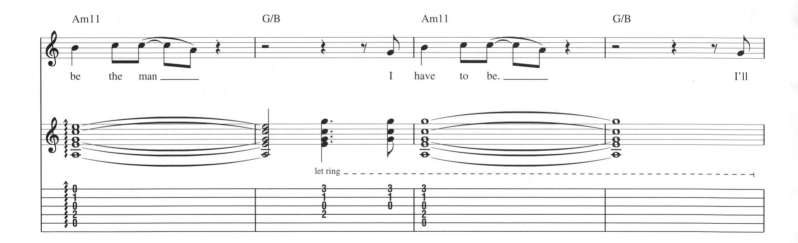

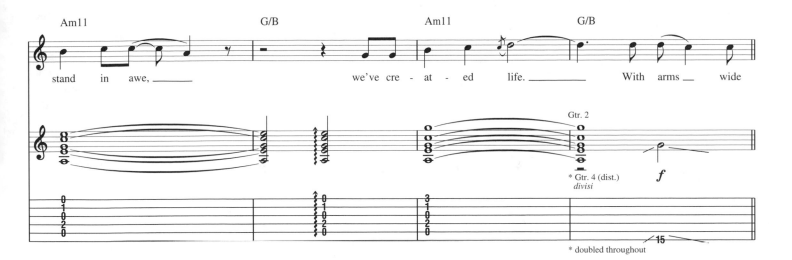

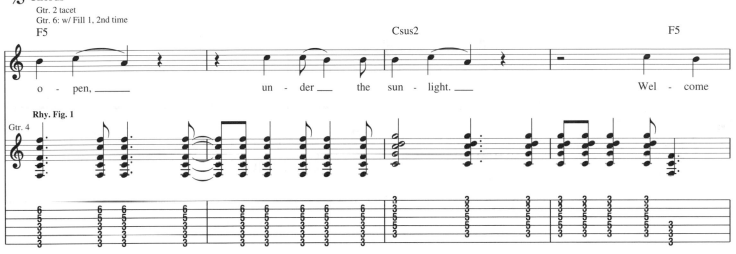

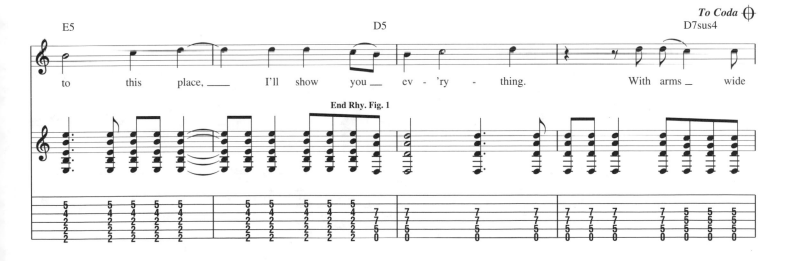

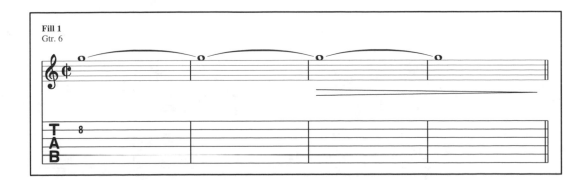

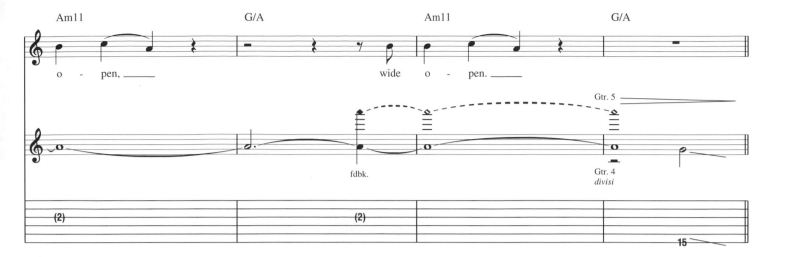

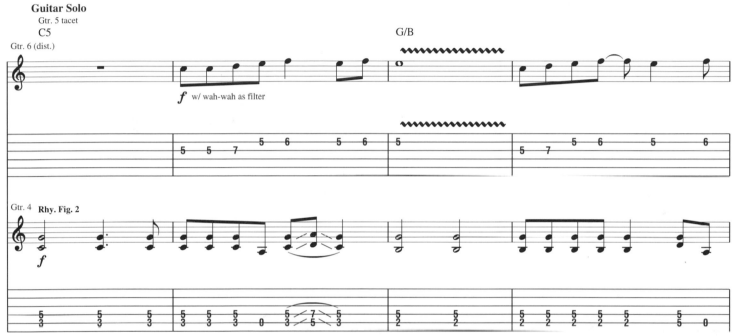

Bridge

Gtr. 4: w/ Rhy. Fig. 2, 2 times, simile

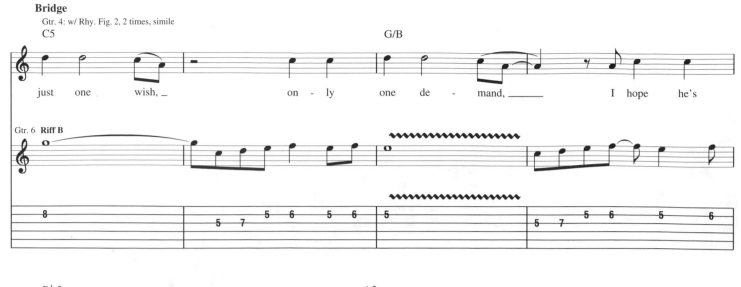

just one wish, _ on-ly one de - mand, _ I hope he's

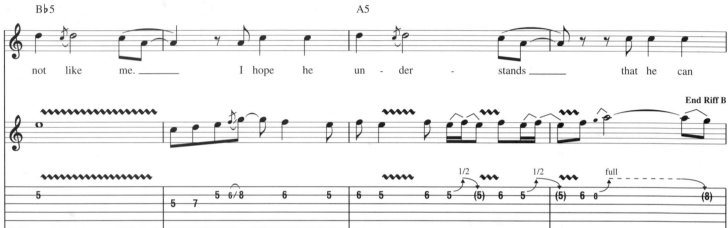

not like me. _ I hope he un - der - stands _ that he can

Gtr. 6: w/ Riff B

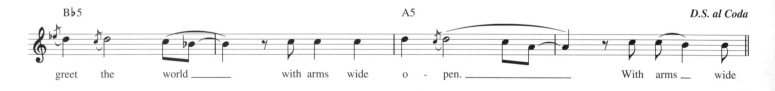

take this life _ and hold it by the hand, _ and he can

greet the world _ with arms wide o - pen. _ With arms _ wide

D.S. al Coda

⊕ *Coda*

Gtr. 4: w/ Rhy. Fig. 1

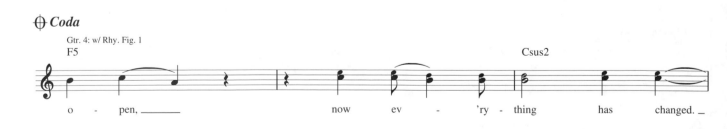

o - pen, _ now ev - 'ry - thing has changed. _

_ I'll show you _ love, _ I'll show you _

50

Higher

Words and Music by Mark Tremonti and Scott Stapp

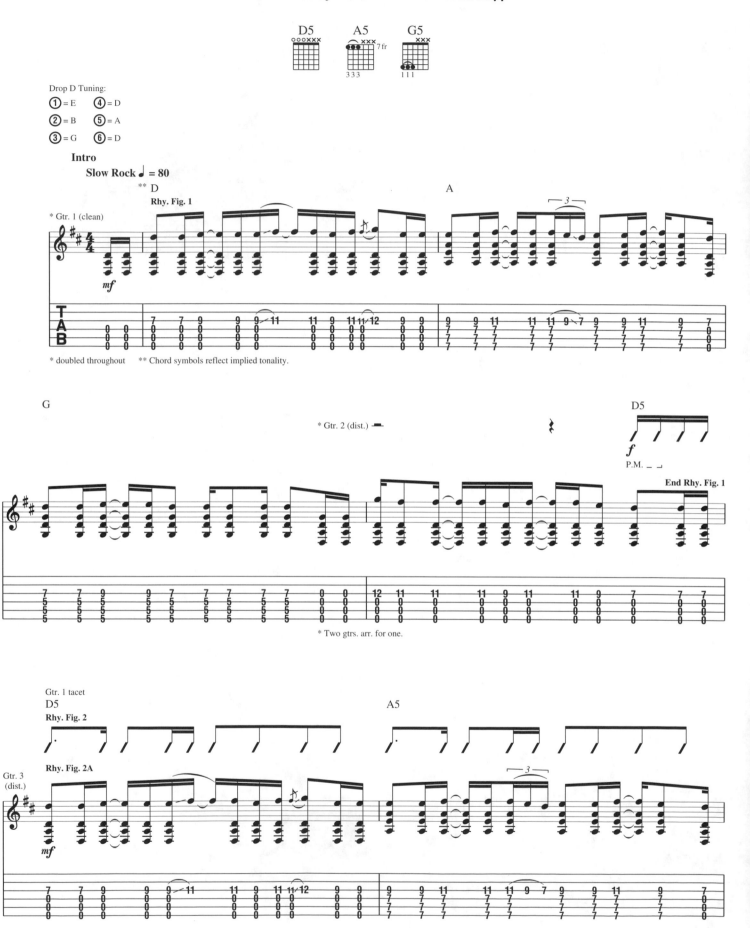

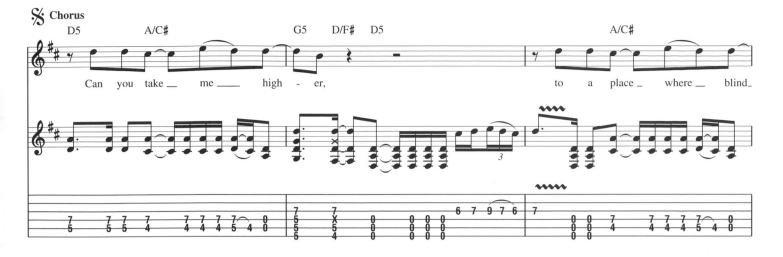

Chorus

Can you take me high-er, to a place where blind

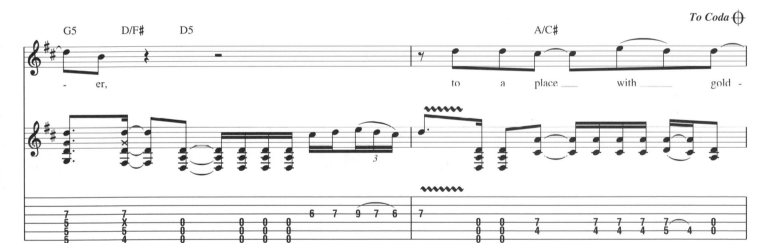

men see?

Can you take me high-

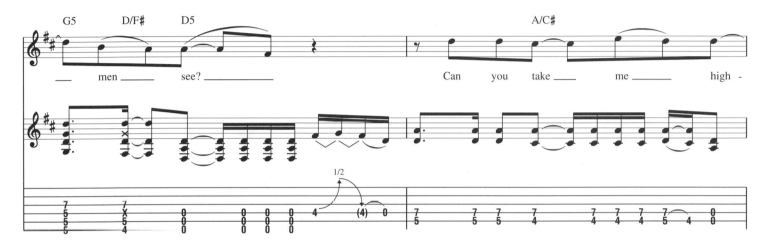

-er, to a place with gold-

To Coda

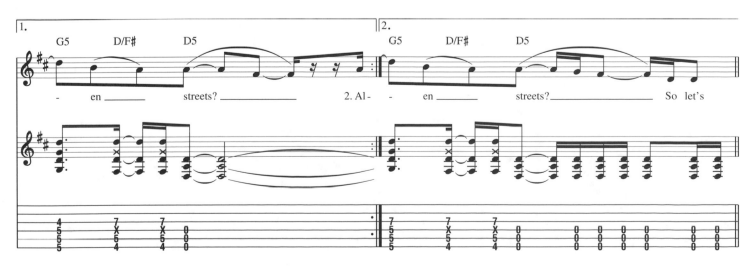

-en streets? 2. Al- -en streets? So let's

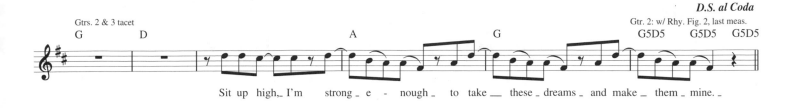

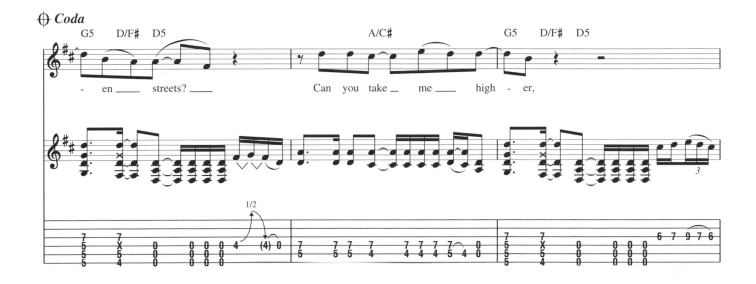

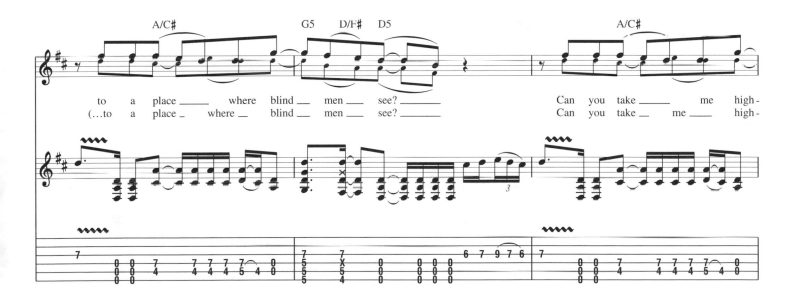

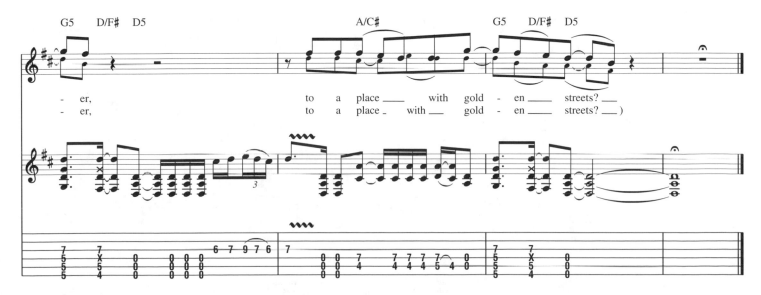

Wash Away Those Years

Words and Music by Mark Tremonti and Scott Stapp

She whis - pered soft - ly _____ to tell _____ a sto - ry _____

a - bout how she had _____ been wronged. _____

As she _____ lay life - less, _____ he stole _____ her in - no - cence,

and this is how she car - ried on. _____

This _____ is how she car - ried on. _____ Well, I

Gtr. 1

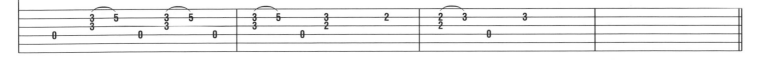

Chorus

Fsus2   D7sus4   Em(♭6)   Em   Gsus2

guess she closed _____ her _____ eyes _____

Rhy. Fig. 1
* Gtrs. 1 & 2 (clean)

mf

let ring throughout

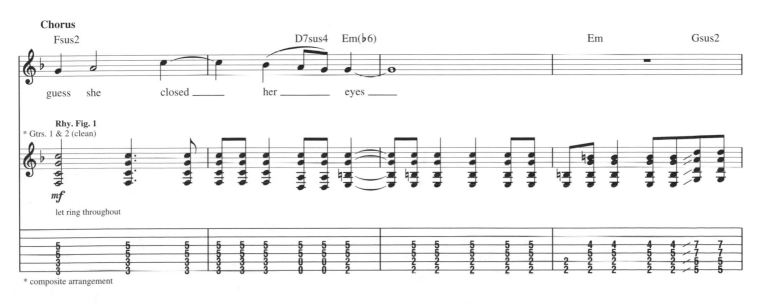

* composite arrangement

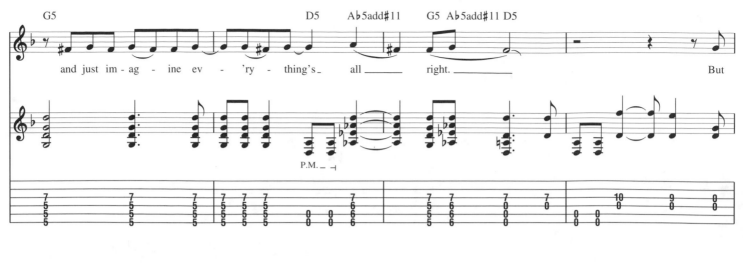

and just im-ag-ine ev-'ry-thing's all _____ right. _____ But

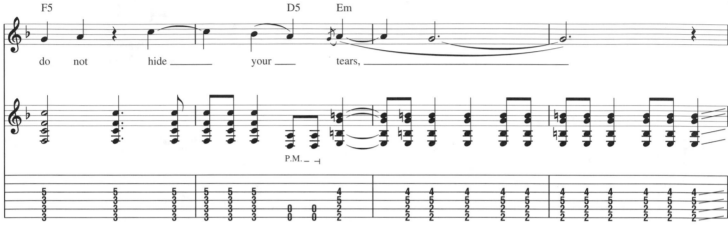

do not hide _____ your _____ tears, _____

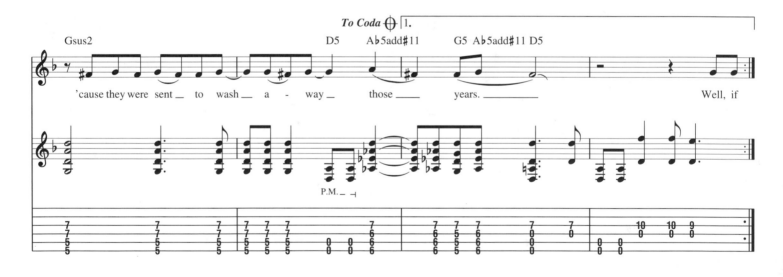

To Coda ⊕ 1.

'cause they were sent _ to wash _ a-way _ those _____ years. _____ Well, if

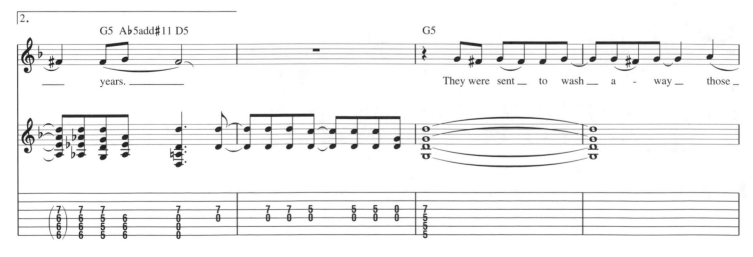

2.

_____ years. _____ They were sent _ to wash _ a-way _ those

years. May-be we can wash a - way those years.

P.M.

Interlude

Rhy. Fig. 2

E♭5

B♭5

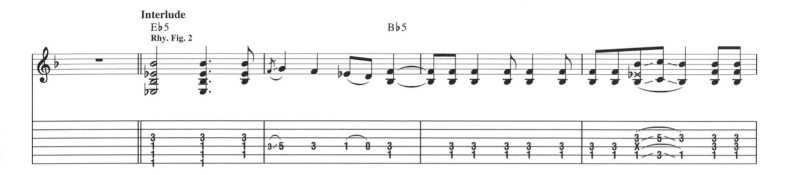

C5   D5 C5   Gsus2   G♭♭♭   Gsus2

For

P.M.

End Rhy. Fig. 2

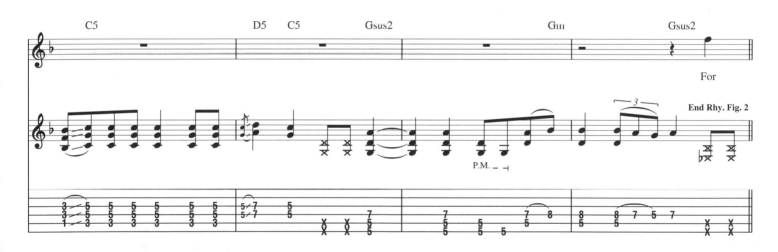

Gtrs. 3 & 4: w/ Rhy. Fig. 2, 1 7/8 times

E♭5   B♭5   C5

we   have   crossed man - y   o -   ceans   and   we   la -   bor

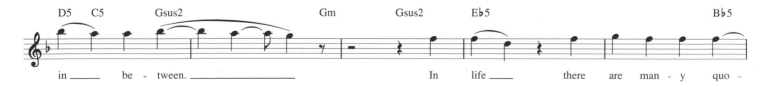

D5 C5   Gsus2   Gm   Gsus2   E♭5   B♭5

in   be - tween.   In   life   there   are   man - y   quo -

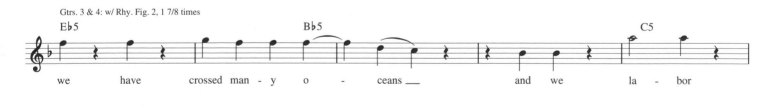

C5   D5 C5   Gsus2   Gm

- tients   and   I   hope   I   find   the   mean,

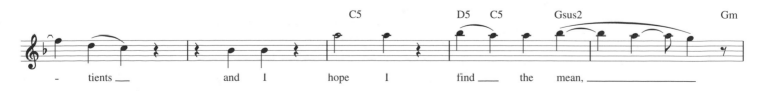

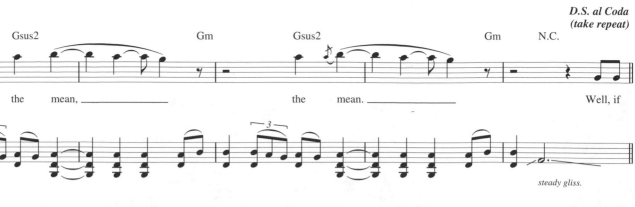

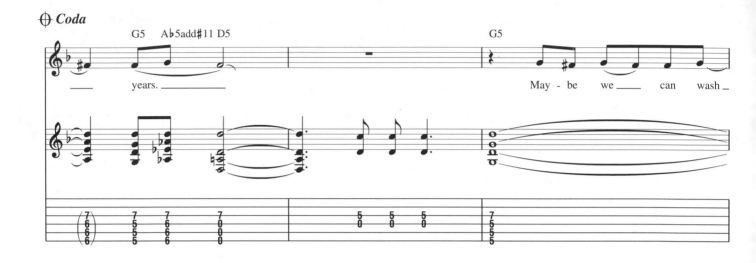

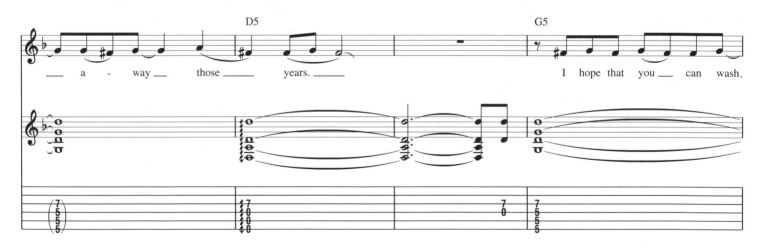

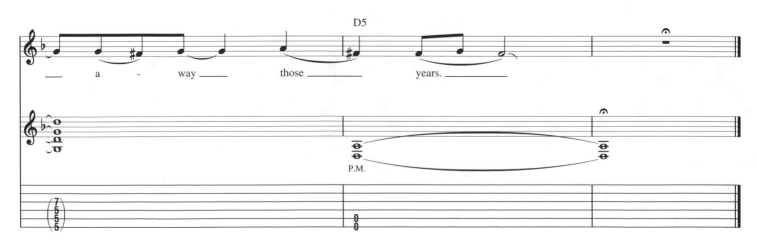

Inside Us All

Words and Music by Mark Tremonti and Scott Stapp

* Key signature denotes D Mixolydian.

** Chord symbols reflect overall tonality.

§ **Chorus**

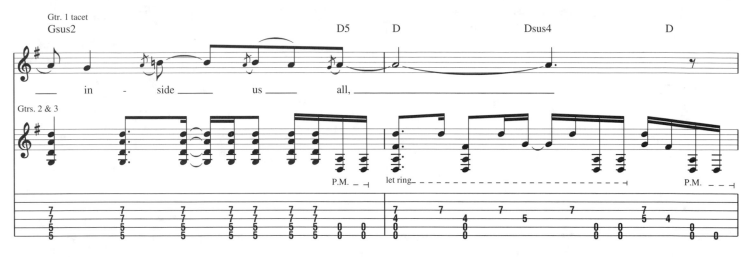

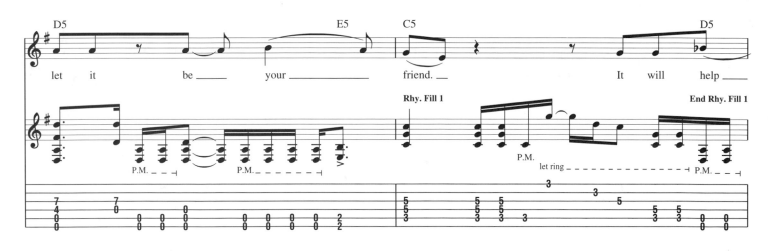

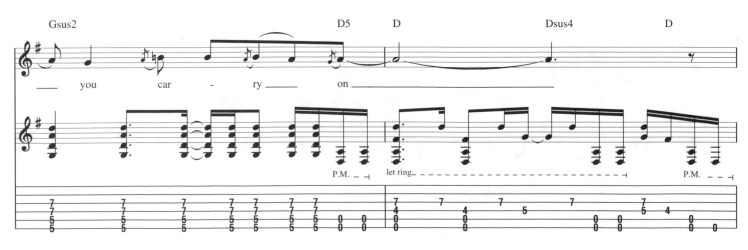

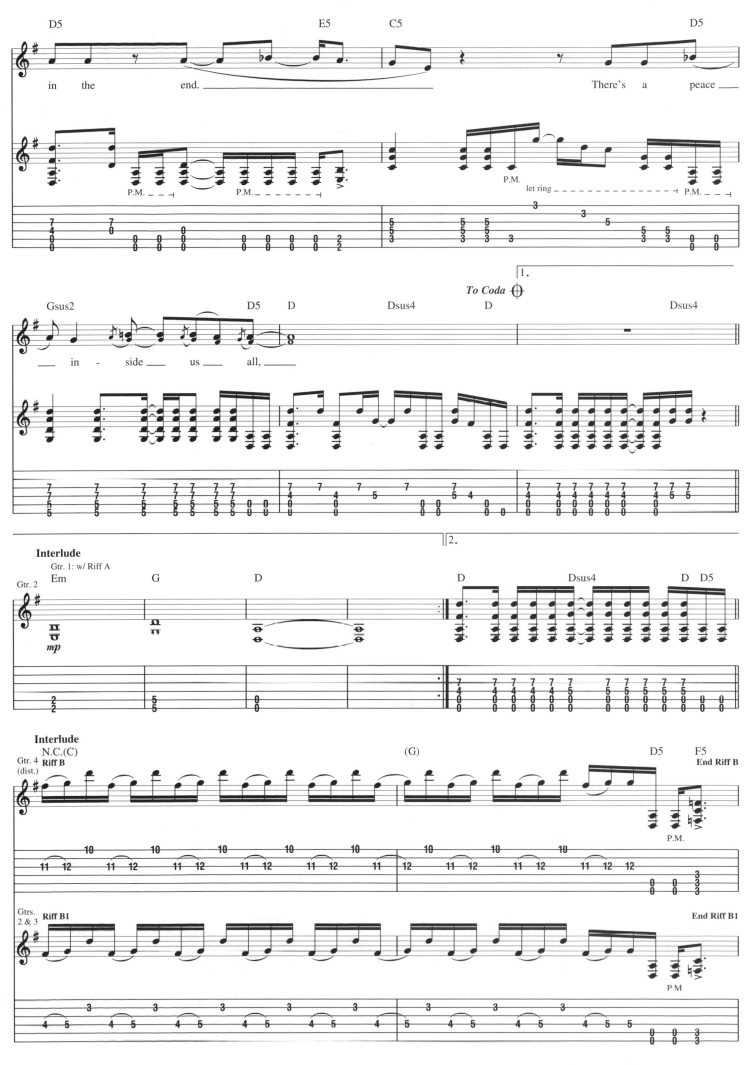

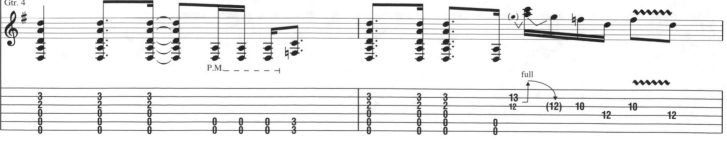

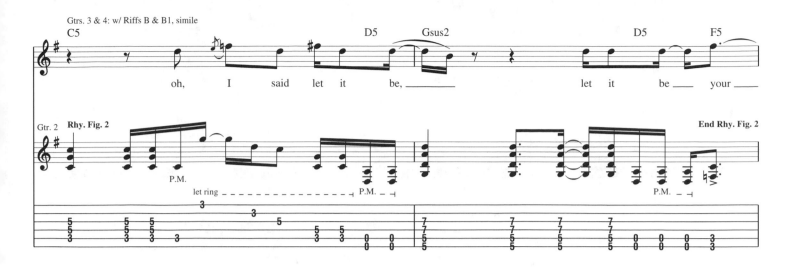

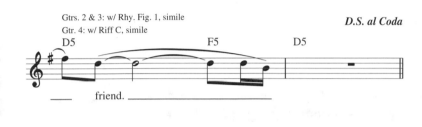

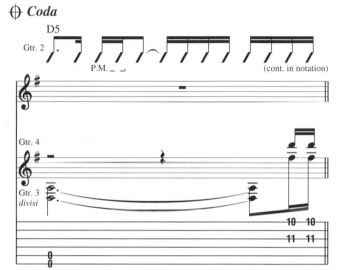

⊕ *Coda*

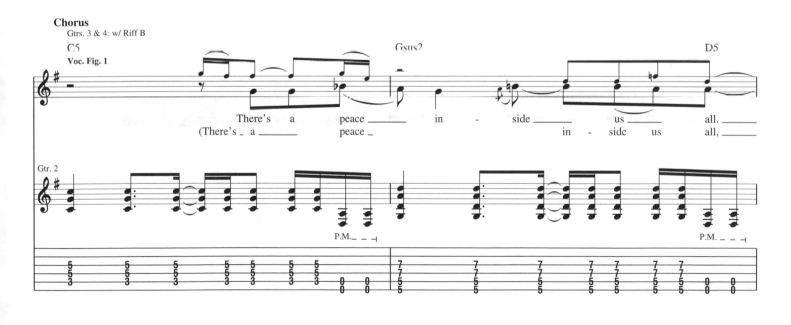

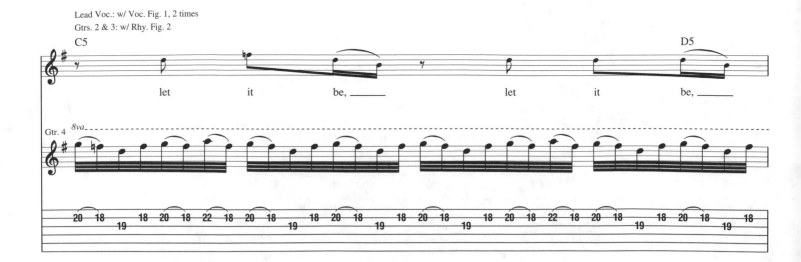

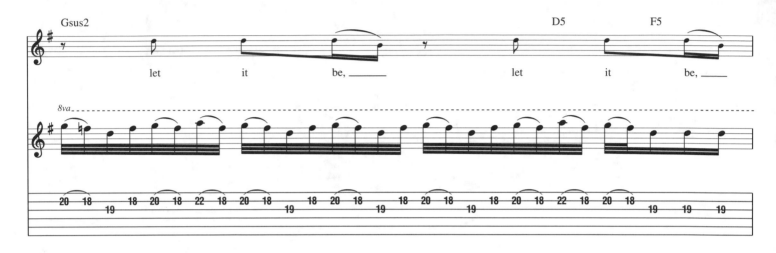

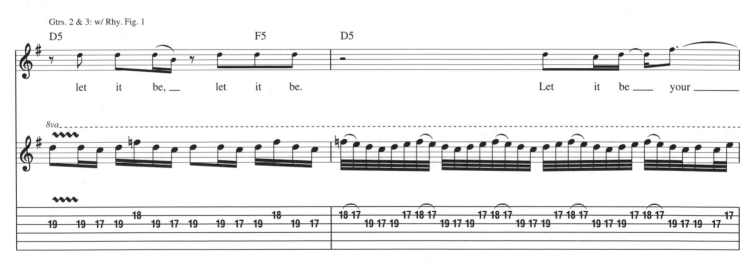

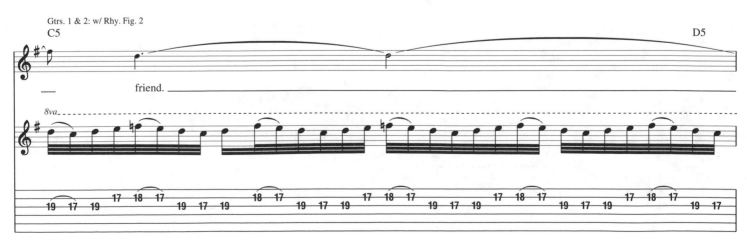

Guitar Notation Legend

Guitar Music can be notated three different ways: on a *musical staff*, in *tablature*, and in *rhythm slashes*.

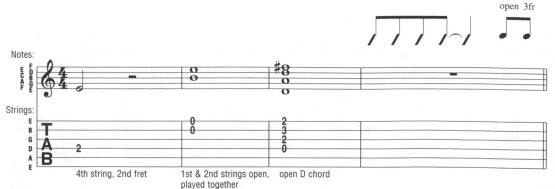

RHYTHM SLASHES are written above the staff. Strum chords in the rhythm indicated. Use the chord diagrams found at the top of the first page of the transcription for the appropriate chord voicings. Round noteheads indicate single notes.

THE MUSICAL STAFF shows pitches and rhythms and is divided by bar lines into measures. Pitches are named after the first seven letters of the alphabet.

TABLATURE graphically represents the guitar fingerboard. Each horizontal line represents a string, and each number represents a fret.

4th string, 2nd fret   1st & 2nd strings open, played together   open D chord

---

HALF-STEP BEND: Strike the note and bend up 1/2 step.

WHOLE-STEP BEND: Strike the note and bend up one step.

GRACE NOTE BEND: Strike the note and bend up as indicated. The first note does not take up any time.

SLIGHT (MICROTONE) BEND: Strike the note and bend up 1/4 step.

BEND AND RELEASE: Strike the note and bend up as indicated, then release back to the original note. Only the first note is struck.

PRE-BEND: Bend the note as indicated, then strike it.

VIBRATO: The string is vibrated by rapidly bending and releasing the note with the fretting hand.

WIDE VIBRATO: The pitch is varied to a greater degree by vibrating with the fretting hand.

HAMMER-ON: Strike the first (lower) note with one finger, then sound the higher note (on the same string) with another finger by fretting it without picking.

PULL-OFF: Place both fingers on the notes to be sounded. Strike the first note and without picking, pull the finger off to sound the second (lower) note.

LEGATO SLIDE: Strike the first note and then slide the same fret-hand finger up or down to the second note. The second note is not struck.

SHIFT SLIDE: Same as legato slide, except the second note is struck.

TRILL: Very rapidly alternate between the notes indicated by continuously hammering on and pulling off.

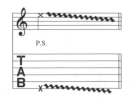

TAPPING: Hammer ("tap") the fret indicated with the pick-hand index or middle finger and pull off to the note fretted by the fret hand.

NATURAL HARMONIC: Strike the note while the fret-hand lightly touches the string directly over the fret indicated.

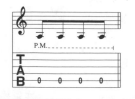

PINCH HARMONIC: The note is fretted normally and a harmonic is produced by adding the edge of the thumb or the tip of the index finger of the pick hand to the normal pick attack.

PICK SCRAPE: The edge of the pick is rubbed down (or up) the string, producing a scratchy sound.

MUFFLED STRINGS: A percussive sound is produced by laying the fret hand across the string(s) without depressing, and striking them with the pick hand.

PALM MUTING: The note is partially muted by the pick hand lightly touching the string(s) just before the bridge.

RAKE: Drag the pick across the strings indicated with a single motion.

TREMOLO PICKING: The note is picked as rapidly and continuously as possible.

VIBRATO BAR DIVE AND RETURN: The pitch of the note or chord is dropped a specified number of steps (in rhythm) then returned to the original pitch.

VIBRATO BAR SCOOP: Depress the bar just before striking the note, then quickly release the bar.

VIBRATO BAR DIP: Strike the note and then immediately drop a specified number of steps, then release back to the original pitch.
